As There As The Sky

By

Dennis Billy

WIPF & STOCK · Eugene, Oregon

Resource Publications
A division of Wipf and Stock Publishers
199 W 8th Ave, Suite 3
Eugene, OR 97401

As There as the Sky
By Billy, Dennis J., CSsR
Copyright©1995 by Billy, Dennis J., CSsR
ISBN 13: 978-1-5326-7080-0
Publication date 9/24/2018
Previously published by Plowman Printing House, 1995

Contents

As There as the Sky

As there as the sky, a me I once
Am touching earth at the edge's why,
Under the day sun's blinding cry;
Then, plummeting toward the milky twi,
Night orbs seize my somber sigh
And turn my piercing stares to the shadow lands:
Beyond my hidden hands,
Beneath the deepest things,
Where souls have wings,
And fly --- just fly.

By the Shore

Every rock
　　　Has a history;
Every shell
　　　A past;
Each grain of sand,
　　　A story to tell
Those who listen
　　　As they pass.

Finger Near the Nigh

Behold, an Unknown Maker,
Finger painting with the clouds
Across the canvassed sky,
Mixes hues of color
Each and all in rich supply.
He fills the scene with Beauty
(As His fingers near the nigh):
A very simple style
From a simple sort of Guy.

Wherever a Snowflake Falls

Wherever a snowflake falls,
Be it the ground
Or the bough of a tree,
Or the top of a mountain,
Or the top of the sea!
Wherever it falls,
Be it even on me!
Be it even the tongue
Or a child in glee!
Wherever it falls
It falls in delight,
For it glistens the sun,
And it whitens the night!
It looks like a star
Coming down from the sky,
And it blows in the wind,
And it wonders the eye!
Wherever it falls
It falls quietly---
Coming, then going,
reminding me, of me.

Even Today

When I was a child
I played by the sea,
And whiled away the day---
Merrily!
I built me a castle
And dug me a moat!
I made me a ship,
And I told it to float!
I picked me a pebble
That washed from a wave,
And polished a pearl
For my pocket to save!
I walked on a stretch
Of yellowish sand,
And found, there, the shore
Of a far away land!

I went with the wind
Wherever it blew!
I followed the birds of the air
As they flew!
I salted the sea!
I named every fish!
I swallowed the sky,
And I made me a wish!
I sat with the shells
When they sang on the shore!
I made peace with the crabs
When they grumbled for war!

But now that I'm old
And wrinkled and gray,
When I go to the sea,
I have little to say.
I sit on a chair,
And I take off my shoes,
And I rest in the sun,
Or I read today's news.
I may have a drink,
If the sun gets too hot.
But, go for a swim?
No, I'd rather not...
But I sometimes remember
Those days with a smile,
When a stone was a jewel,
and a step was a mile,
When a mound was a mountain,
and a puddle, the sea,
When the sky could be touched,
And when I could be me!
For a child subsists
On laughter and joy---
To him, everything
Is a game or a toy!
His world is a world
Of wonder and play,
And that has a place in my heart---
Even today!

Plankton

The sea is filled with tiny things
That play upon the waves,
Small, shining things that eat the sun
By soaking up its rays.
Alive they float until some fish
Goes fishing for its stew;
When dried and cooked that tasty fish
Becomes the tish of you!

A Rummaging Mosquito

A rummaging mosquito
Came a rummaging for blood:
He rummaged in the summer heat;
He rummaged in the mud.
And then he rummaged on my skin
And raised his mighty spud,
Then stuck it deeply in and out
Before my thumb could thud.

A Poem

Here I lie before your heavy eyes
            --- the gibberish of a foolish man,
Who thinks that he can in a rhyme
        Portray a mood or freeze a time,
Who feels that Day, the early Morn,
        Can come alive in written form.

And he has surely failed---
        No matter how a word is chosen,
            It must remain frozen
                On the printed page
                    From age to age.
But Day once full of gleaming light
Must end its reign and turn to Night!
And Morning slips away too soon;
The Sun moves on it turns to noon!

Here I lie before your heavy eyes
                    ---the gibberish of a foolish man.
When Life with all its ebbs and flows
        Keeps changing seasons and colors,
I know that I'll remain right here
        With wrinkled corners and finger smears.

But before I return to where I belong,
        A simple thing remains for which I long.
Please, in thoughtful times when you are all alone,
        Remember I exist--- a sad poor poem!
And if, though meter poor and ill-matched rhymes
        Are cast throughout my every line,
I might, perchance, live in your mind:
        Oh please! If you would be so kind!

If Vibrant Life cannot find home in me
        Perhaps your living memory
                Can set me free
From this dead white leaf made of a tree.
And then I will no longer be
                    ---the gibberish of a foolish man,
but the living voice of an wishful fan!

wily willie while

wily willie while was a lazy sort of child,
who idled all his whiles, while he whiled away the day.
he lived on a small isle (scarcely longer than a mile)
where he idled all his whiles, while he whiled away the day.
wily willie whiled in his own private sort of way:
he never whiled wild, seldom ever idled riled,
but whiled with a smile, for it was his chosen style
to idle all his whiles, while he whiled away the day.

while whiling away the day one day, wily willie while
whiled a certain child, one wild millie while (no relation),
who, all the while, whiled wily willie while he whiled her
in his own private sort of way (i.e., a while with a smile).
it was love at first while on this small isle
(scarcely long than a mile), and, after a while,
They walked down the aisle and had a while and a while and a
        while,
while they idled all their whiles, while they whiled away the day.
and soon wily willie's isle could hardly hold the many whiles
while they whiled away the day.
and poor willie while whiled wild, whiled riled without a smile,
for his whiles always idled while he whiled away the day,
and they whiled while he idled in his own private sort of way.

Napoleon at Waterloo

The tumored rectum agonized his goals;
With tender crotch it rubbed upon his rolls.
As fill of pain began to wane his greed,
And scratching caused his sitting vein to bleed,
His might horse unsaddled he from fate,
"I'll fight the battle on another date!"
(The rest, of course, is history.)
More troops brought in the British through the night;
The French all wished to flee (their tongues tight).
On battleground (The very next today),
His men retreated frantic from the fray.
The time he wasted more than less had meant
Disaster which he could not circumvent.
And so his dream for Europe fell to void:
His army, dead and scattered, was destroyed.

Moral: Let not posterity await
            Posteriority and date.

If

If earth is just a tiny sphere
That pivots on a string,
And goes about the sun each year
To make the winter spring,
I wonder what such knowledge tells
Me of the race of man,
Who fights his wars and battles
On a ball so small in plan?

Upon the Shore

Before the sea upon the shore,
Where Cicero, in times of yore,
Did drill his tongue with scraps of pebbled ore,
I couraged up my gums to girt
And furthermored my talent to assert.
Enclosed I swollen grains between my lips;
I balanced on my teeth phonetic tips;
I diaphramed my lungs with foreign words;
I blasted rhyming riddles to the birds!
Yet when I muttered once a silent sound
That sent my tonsils twitching round and round,
I lost the soiled mouthful through the throat:
My stomach, churned and spoiled, lost its coat.
Now I sit upon the porcelain throne,
Consuming pitless prunes, ungraveling the groan,
Besetting not so much upon the getting of vowels,
But more concerned this moment with the movement of my
        bowels.

Treason God Forgot

So subtle is the devil and the manner of his ways:
He often makes a muddle of man's seasons, years and days.
He walks about unnoticed (as silent as a spy)
In search of cracks to cranny in, to grind his teeth and pry.

He stalks unseen in caverns deep, beneath all conscious thought,
While unsuspecting man mistakes his evil for an ought.
In argument and art, they say, his craft is truly strong:
A right he'll take, manipulate, and turn into a wrong.
Deception is his only tool, which very few resist
(Especially since very few believe him to exist).
From morning, noon till night again retreats into the dawn,
He'll hook ensnare, delude, entrap, and not so much as yawn.
He wants to move man like a pawn, a puppet on a string,
That would perform his every wish without an uttering.
His single ploy is to destroy then coil all that is
Around his slimy skin and make it all, quite simply, "his."
His trickery and sheer deceit betray what he is not,
And what he is is nothing more than treason God forgot.

The Me-Me's

The world is filled with me-me souls
Believing no one save themselves,
Half-witted fools who think they're whole,
Because they've stocked their ballast shelves
With plastic things that beep and squeak
Beneath the fog that's in the leak.
Amid the noise that numbs the notch,
Nor do they danger comprehend
Within their yacht without a watch
That rusts and rocks without an end,
Because the wash-waves wear and tear
Beyond what keels can seem to bear.
Though others holler out their lungs
With sounds that make their tonsils twitch,
No screech can reach from any tongue
To pierce the plastic things with which
The me-me's occupy themselves
Throughout their little lives like elves.
As time ticks through its lasting tock
And marches in the muddy marsh,
The me-me's mark a change in stock.

In that they lose their hollow hearts,
For now they too just beep and squeak
Beneath the fog that's in the leak
That steals the souls that make them speak
Beyond what plastic things can reck.

Bonfire

Blazing-burn!
Licking night in endless turn---
Yearn!
Thrusting tongues in ceaseless wear,
Lapping up tasteless air!
Mightily it roars! Soar
Above the oak and pine,
Blazing-blind with crackling whine!
A thousand glistening eyes
Watch its captivating dance
With the stars of the sky;
Five hundred wandering hearts---
A sigh.
The sparkling sight begins to die.
Why?
Smouldering charcoal on the ground---
Sizzling sound---
Pound.

trapeze

swinging in
the rhythm of
a catch,
one leaps in-
side him-
self;
another smiles
with a certain gravity.

The Crows

Listen, or the crows will caw
      Then swoop,
While chickens slumber
      In their coop,
Unto the field
      To peck up
Grain for grain
      (as if a law unto themselves)
The yield---
      Not to mention the many cattle.

cain

Be starved in i
as-ha!-sin-ate
my brother-brain
e-n-t-r-a-i-l-e-d---
he wailed the sky
with smoke...
...turned red,
refused to keep/
u-n-k-e-p-t. un-
Abled-dead, he
stained the sod;
Be marked my head to Nod:
"ca(i)nnot-Be-come-un-clod,"
me fled...
"may-not-Be-sod,"
Be bled...

Ockham's Child

I
often
wonder
about
God's
thunder,

should
he
utter
with
a
stutter,

a
"not-
not"
for
a
"not."

in-the-snow-by-night

he tracks a trail
of melting tracks---
deer-in-the-snow-by-night---
the thaw of winter's sun, the creaking trees,
in SIGHT!
a bullet to his gun,
the greatest ease,
SqUeEzE TIGHT!
BLEED, BLED, BLOOD
upon the snow,
the mud, out of breath,
BrEaThE DEATH-------------------------------
in-the-snow-by-night.

Exposed

Left upon the barren hills to cry unwanted,
Beyond the chills of night, the day now daunted,
Unfortunate Life! Elemental Strife!
Abandoned to Not by Beasts of Prey!
Rent apart! Will rot! --- Decay!
Becoming till-not-living --- Clay!

A feast this day for the powers of Lethe,
For a beast will weigh the hours of Death!
"Unworthy of Life are they unwanted!
Off to the hills where wolves wait gaunted,
Smacking their hungry teeth and tongues
For the flesh and blood of these little ones!"

Tomorrow is not yet today;
The past is present to stay;
And the heart of man is haunted
With the cold night's chill,
And the wild wolves' hunger to kill,
And the child's voice echoing the hill --- Unwanted!

Mourning

The tower tolls a somber march in time,
a dismal dirge, a melancholic whine.
The ground receives my disbelieving stare,
A lifeless friend below --- I tarry there.
Descending down from darkness to the earth,
My penetrating glance itself asserts.
Upon the mound, my poorly tended trust
Peers through the putrefaction and the dust.

When Weak, Forsaken

When weak, forsaken man has weathered strife,
And gathered round him travellers to God,
When finished be his lonesome road through life,
With broken staff and faltering facade,
Upon what path will destiny declare
His ventured life unlived, his dismal death unsung,
Before what sight will dying man despair,
Or otherwise believe he heaven won?
A quest unsought encounters human will;
Man's flesh with spirit yearns approaching day.
Such knowledge night awakens; dreams fulfill.
And man, the poet of his own dismay,
Finds death diminished by a burning star,
Beholds his journey end from afar.

The Traveller's Rest

Far have I come this day,
From there, beyond the ridge
As far as eye can see.
Every step, half taken,
Half left behind;
Every path not chosen---
Now lost in memory---
Brings my journey here.

Far have I come,
Through thicket and through fog,
Over mountain fastness,
In the mud and in the bog.
Far have I come---
A lonely traveller,
Foraging for rest
Beneath the restless sky.

Now my journey dwindles to a step,
As aching limbs and back,
Soreness of foot, each breath,
The pain of miles travelled,
And of miles yet to come,
The sweat---
All bid my bones
The peace of traveller's rest.

There, by the wayside,
My home will be this night---
With staff beside the fire
And head beneath the stars.
Silently the night will carry rest,
Until the darkness turns to dawn,
And the morning sun sheds its solitary light
Upon my chosen path.

Now, at this quiet hour,
When shadows cast no more
And darkness covers day,
I remember moments passing
And think of moments yet to come---
Moments which speak of my journey,
Which dwindle to a breath
And bring my weariness rest.

Heavy the lid falls upon the eye,
As the mind returns to dreaming,
As the soul becomes the sky.
Asleep in sleep, I wander
Through a thousand journeys,
To a thousand wayside places,
To a thousand unknown destinations---
And a single rude awakening.

Life is a journey, as is death---
And man the traveller.
His every breath, a step;
His every step, the breath of a journey ended:
Night dwindles into dawn,
The day into dusk, the journey into the traveller's rest,
The traveller into his final hour.

when i no longer be

when i no longer be,
when from my body free,
go down to the sea
and watch for me---
i will be there,
everywhere,
aware.

see me in the waves
as they crash upon the sand,
snatching polished pebbles
and broken shells
off to foreign lands.

hear me in the wind
as it sets the scene with clouds,
serenading the setting sun
and strumming the colored strings of sky
with the whistle of its wandering why.

smell me in the air
as it fills your expanding lungs
with the salty sea,
and sends the seagulls soaring high
to be one with the crystalline bowl of sky.

taste me in the ocean mist
as it lingers on your thirsting tongue,
salted with a double portion
of my spirit
and soul.

feel me in the smooth, wet sand
as it molds its solitary grains
to the curvatures of your feet,
and takes from you your precious prints---
the momentary traces of immortality.

when i no long be,
when from my body free,
go down to the sea
and watch for me.
I will be there,
everywhere,
aware---
silently watching for you.

Ode to a Friend

Down beneath the sodded ground your body now does lie,
       Cold and pale, withered and still.
The somber land swallows you up beyond recognition
       As you become the dirt upon which we once walked.
So short a time to live--- a life of thwarted hopes and ambitions
       Receiving so little change for fruition!
Is this the path we all must brave before we are
       Beckoned to the sullen grave?
Does life upon this cold-hearted earth deny us
       Even that little mirth to be gained from our own fulfilled
aspirations
I pray, God--- No!

Yet, how many seasons must sorrowfully pass before
       Even the memory of my dear friend has fled the minds of
          those concerned
And must take up with the night wind in search of place to rest?
And how long before it too must die?

O Friend! I do remember!
But in a single moment's passing I too must join Death's ugly
       ranks.
And Nature's way which hounded you will surely do the same.
What then will become of your desperate plea?
The scratched-out markings on this page will never
       Conquer Time's ceaseless wear.
Will you simply fade away?
Will we simply decay into the earthen parts of which we are
       made?

O mirthless dirt below my feet of ages past and gone,
You bear the trodden spoils of countless numbers harmed!
Of noble Caesar no more remains but sun bleached bones of
      white;
His flesh once full of might and fight became the worm's delight.
Of Helen, Ah yes! Royal visage of a thousand ships from hoistec
      sails to hull,
Now only slimy snakes attracts to coil in her skull.
And Xerxes' own immortal guard which once scourged all the Eas
Decayed beneath your royal turf, is now your land's own feast.

But mirthless dirt you conquer not only corpses of those known
      and great,
The rotting flesh of leper men, who wallowed in their lives,
Now settles down below your sands--- But at least they were men
And what of this, here, in my hand?
What name had he or she?
Dying soldier? Peasant old? Forgotten? Unknown like you and
      me?
And what of this here?
In what noble part did you once dwell?
A heavy heart? A vibrant limb? A turned cheek?

Out across the somber plain I see, my Friend,
So many restless spirits begging to be let free from Nature's
      wearing ways;
To be reborn, to feel once more the simple pleasures of
      A life too soon deprived.
But the cries are hidden--- locked up within
      The very stones which mark these dreary graves.
And who will free them from the dust whence they came and hav
      returned?
And who will comfort them in their earthen cells?

But what is this, my Friend, sprouting up from
        A corner of your barren bed?
A small, just budding flower, arrayed in white and gold.
Its name escapes me this moment, yet I have seen it many times
        before.
It is a pretty thing--- and it is alive--- soaking up
        The precious foods of Life.
Life and Death, Death and Life--- the questions remain
        unanswered.
But existing in the very midst of Death this small, stubborn
        Thread of Life,
And on the deep ocean of anxiety and despair, this one
        Driftwood of Hope.
O Friend! May this tiny blossom keep us both afloat,
And perhaps one day we will frolic and play---
        ---As in better days.

Your Dreadful Hand

Your dreadful hand, O Death, lays hold the vagaries of men;
Your empty dark of night, their spirits fear and fold.
Silent are the voices calling, empty the stars that shine;
Turbulent the waves that crash and crush the rock.
For man, the journey dwindles to your solitary grasp;
His breath once breathed in breath now memory bequeathes.
Scattered are his dreams once dreamed in youth;
Battered are his bones by truth and useless age.
O what in man becomes the dreadful calming of your hand?
Upon what leg to stand will, dying, he reply?
Perish the tears and grief allowed to fall!
Muster the worm and wage the broken sod!
Beckon the years! And take to God your touch!
Behold your vagaries, O Death! Amidst the thunderous gloom---
        Man will defy!

Biding Time

One old man's make-believing sighs
Of faded youth and times gone by,
Speak in endless rhythm to the rockings of his chair,
Composing hymns of silence to quiet his despair.
Between each heavy rock descends a token from the past,
Which sits beside his aged friend to tend him till his last
Breath of air,
When he leaves his rocking chair,
And ascends to where?
To where?

Until that time when time, like wine
From grape, takes on a different shape,
His memories will come and go,
March fast and slow,
Entertain his soul
Till church bells toll.
And he, to earth below,
Will sleep in the turbulence of his grave,
Becoming wind and wave;
To master worm, a slave,
Until the day when nothing sighs
From the box once fitted to his size,
And a still small voice from heaven cries,
"Arise, my son, Arise!"

The Shelter

Bared against the rock---
                    The naked rock;
Head upon breast
                    'Neath Heaven's smile;
Breath upon breath
                    From lonely miles walked:
Two friends, their God,
                    A mountain's peak---
Their troubled spirits turn
                    And speak;
A tranquil soul
                    Is born.

The Priest

Late one night I turned my heavy head
Toward the shadows of my lonely bed.
A melting silence fell on me and said,
"Alone you live, abandoned, left for dead."

Head to hands I dropped in fear;
I listened with a quiet tear,
Then felt the stillness swelling near,
"But I am here, I am here."

Within A Hovel

Within a hovel by a lonely cave
There lived a beggar clothed in tattered gray.
When wind and rain unclad his smelly hide,
And drenched him cold with nothing warm inside,
He hungered for a bit of bread or broth,
But tasted lips instead and filthy froth.
When thunder sent a crashing through his head
And ostracized his skin and scalp with dread,
He shivered as a chill shot up his spine
And wallowed on the ground in silent whine.
When villagers betook him for a fool
And shook his ears with limpid ridicule,
He wiped his cheek and breathed a breathy sigh,
Then turned his stare toward them and wondered why.
But who, in truth, the naked beggar be?
Perhaps he is what no one here can see.
Through frailty his blood and bone bewailed,
Though loneliness his sickly lungs exhaled,
He found within this hovel by a cave
A laurel men have not but surely crave.
For poverty and lack for him did win
A smile on his lips deep down within,
And when he died he reveled in delight,
For through the cave he passed--- a noble knight.

Grace

Late at night, after
the common prayer, when the monks,
weary as they said, follow their
divergent paths
and leave their habits for
bed, I go beyond the brick of
cloister walk to a place
by a lake
where the wind blows cool upon
my face, and the water falls at
quiet pace upon the shore.
There, the moon gives
light to faded memories, the stars
whine within, I loosen my
collar more,
fall in upon the grass
and ponder the milky white way,
having nothing to say
but softly,
"Grace, I thank you for
Life," so softly, "Grace, Your wonders
are rife."

Parting Steps

As we, once gathered,
Silently depart,
And travel separate ways
Before us into life,
Allow us time to ponder
Ere we go--- to bid, "Farewell."
For long has been the time
Since when we first began,
And, while together, close became
Each traveller to each.
With now our journey ended,
As parting moments come,
The task of leaving beckons forth
The heart's impassioned cry.

And with our grief awakened,
Once silent tears are shed,
And close embraces shared,
Such times, as when
We gathered, will be lost.
Our journey will have ended,
But we, on solitary paths,
Arrived--- with parting steps.

In Silence

When what once yearned for
Dwindles far from want,
As wings span high
And eagles sear the sun,
The dream now lived
In silence with the night,
Becomes the burning fire
Of a deeper quest.

Bending Wood

A bending tree, to Thee
My soul doth bow,
For Thou in me doth water
Turn to sap.

Throughout these limbs
Thy silent flow extends:
From ground to root,
From root to tree.

So far from Thee
These branches stretch,
These longing leaves
Unfold.

So near to Thee
Thy light descends,
And bends with
Bending wood.

Secret Stars

I must inside myself concealed
To see if moments trickle down with time,
Articulate a silent task,
Or wander with a whine;
If none exist or from within reply,
Without I stand till ponder fills the sky:
Beneath, above, beyond my reach
Sheer shining stars supply
The yearning of a distant swell,
The wonder of a sigh.

hearing

interior tones of silence
swell upon my inner

H... E... A... R...
DIALOGUING WITH SELF...
CONVERSING WITH OTHER...
BECOMING ONE

with near-
&
where am i other-

I... N... G...?

LiFe

LIFE

        (That uncoNTAINAble swELL
        of siLent SEEm-LiKe-seeMING:
        SPRingING oUt of the TElling-well;
        REAMing WhcrE tHE WATERS dwELL
        RipE witH riFLED dREAMing)
                      ABOUNDS!

      It rushes with the waifing wind---
Wake, wallow, whim, whiff, whine!
        Tympanic rhythm---
      Twine!
Strewn, straight, straggle...
                    Sin...
             Seminal sign---
                    Vine

of the LIVING BREAD!
stirring the dead from their rotting bed;
FLESH to their brittle bones will WED!
so it is said of StRiFe:
"TO LIFE! TO LIFE!"

solitude

        sojourning with self
           in silence,
        communing with life
           in death...

                    ...listening to around,
                      finding abound...

then taking another
    breath...

The Mystic

The Word captures..........me..................

The Mystery escapes...............me..........

The skeleton remains.............................